CW00967895

AN ATTEMPT TO DESCRIBE

HAFOD

at Hafod Cardigan Shire
16 Sept 1786

AN ATTEMPT TO DESCRIBE
HAFOD

by

George Cumberland

A BICENTENARY EDITION

Edited and Introduced by

Jennifer Macve and Andrew Sclater

Illustrated
with drawings from a sketchbook of Thomas Jones of Pencerrig
introduced by Donald Moore

Ymddiriedolaeth Yr Hafod - Hafod Trust

Published by the Hafod Trust
Obtainable from
J. Macve
3 Trefor Road
Aberystwyth
Ceredigion
SY23 2EH

This edition first published 1996.

ISBN: 0 9527941 0 1

Acknowledgements:
"An Attempt to Describe Hafod" is reproduced from a copy at the National Library of Wales, by kind permission of the Library.
The Thomas Jones drawings are reproduced by kind permission of the owner, and by arrangement with the Friends of Hafod.

Printed in Wales by
The National Library of Wales.

INTRODUCTION

A BICENTENARY EDITION

This publication celebrates the 200th anniversary of the first work to give a detailed, eye-witness account of the Cardiganshire estate of Hafod. Under the ownership of Thomas Johnes, Hafod achieved supreme status as a landscape of the Picturesque in the late eighteenth century.

Cumberland's book did much to popularise Hafod and Devil's Bridge amongst tourists in search of the Picturesque, many of whom later acknowledged their debt to him when publishing their own guides or descriptive tours. His text, reproduced here in facsimile, combines romantic language with accurate topographical observation, to great effect. The 1796 book was illustrated with a single map, but the present edition is complemented by drawings, made at Hafod in 1786 by Thomas Jones, many of which have not previously been published.

Cumberland's text is divided into five unnumbered chapters. The first introduces the reader to Hafod and sets it in context, geographically and aesthetically. The remaining chapters describe each of the walks, in turn. Two are circuit walks around the demesne, beginning and ending at the mansion; they were referred to by William Gilpin as 'the *lady's-walk*, a circuit of about three miles - and the *gentleman's-walk*, about six', though Cumberland did not employ these names.[1]

The Lady's Walk, for the most part on gentle gradients, followed a course through woodland and meadow to the north of the River Ystwyth, which constitutes the 'backbone' of the designed landscape. A diversion from this walk towards Cwmystwyth, described as the New Walk, remained unfinished until 1805.

1

The longer Gentleman's Walk was a more challenging circuit, exploring the steep hillside and tributary valleys to the south of the river and offering magnificent views over Hafod's 'variegated' landscape. This circuit was reached by crossing the Ystwyth at the Alpine Bridge, which Johnes rebuilt at least once. The Gentleman's Walk returned to the mansion by way of a 'long flying bridge' across the river, probably a rickety timber affair – picturesque to behold and terrifying to cross. Such a bridge was illustrated by Mrs Stackhouse at Downton; like Hafod's flying bridge, it has long since disappeared.[2]

The fourth walk, along the dramatic wooded gorge west of Pontrhydygroes, lay outside Hafod's boundary and was subsequently removed from the itinerary of walks available to visitors. The final chapter is devoted to portraying the sublime landscape of the Rheidol and Mynach ravines at Devil's Bridge. Here Johnes had erected a superbly situated inn, the Hafod Arms, and over the following two decades he was to have the satisfaction of seeing it thronged each summer with tourists, eager to experience for themselves the picturesque scenes so evocatively described by George Cumberland.[3]

THE PICTURESQUE AND PICTURESQUE TOURISM

The Picturesque is a genre in the history of designed landscape. Coming to the fore in the 1790s, when few prudent landowners were executing large-scale landscape schemes, it is more readily studied in contemporary theory than in physical landscapes.[4] The great pioneer of the new aesthetic was the Reverend William Gilpin (1724-1804), whose theories of the Picturesque were formulated in relation to the composition of paintings and drawings. Gilpin's publications provided a didactic framework by which he instructed his readers how to look at and appreciate natural scenery.[5] His various Tours (published as *Observations on the...* [e.g. *River Wye*] from 1782 to 1809), contain critical appreciations and often suggest ways in which the artist might rearrange real scenery on paper or canvas to achieve a more perfect approximation to a picturesque ideal than the unaltered view could provide.

The concave mirror known as the Claude Glass was an essential accessory to the artist in search of the Picturesque, for it offered a means of manipulating perspective and reducing the width of a scene that it might be 'condensed' into an image.[6] Gilpin specified requirements for the component parts of picturesque scenes. His specifications include the broad principles that a view should have foreground side screens (to act as a 'natural' internal frame), with middle ground and background of differing shades. However, he also indicated a hierarchy of Picturesqueness, with subjects such as ruins and humble cottages more picturesque than monuments and mansions. Farm animals were considered picturesque also, but for Gilpin there were right and wrong ways of disposing them within a scene, and the number shown in the picture was also significant.[7]

Towards the end of the eighteenth century, war on the continent made foreign travel dangerous. At the same time, less money was available for the rich to visit France and Italy. The Grand Tour was much less often undertaken than in the days of their predecessors. In Britain, however, a wealthy merchant class was developing, and the economic advances due to industrialisation and agricultural improvement led to the development of safer and better public roads. The first phase of Picturesque tourism coincides with these social and physical changes. Gilpin was the primary guide, and taking his *Tours*, visitors flocked to the Lake District, the Wye Valley, and to

Scotland. By 1800, a circular tour of the whole of Wales was becoming popular, with a visit to Hafod and Devil's Bridge as an essential component.

THOMAS JOHNES OF HAFOD - BEAUTIFYING ORIGINAL WILDNESS

Thomas Johnes (1748-1816) was the son of a Welsh squire, Thomas Johnes (d. 1780) and his wife, Elizabeth (née Knight), of Croft Castle, Herefordshire.[8] His childhood in northern Herefordshire, among the ancient trees of Croft, is likely to have been significant in framing his clear love of landscape. Nearby his cousin, Richard Payne Knight (1750-1824), began planting his celebrated Downton Vale around 1772. Another neighbour, Uvedale Price (1747-1829), was active in remodelling his own landscape at Foxley, throughout the same decade.[9] Price and Knight together became the major theorists of Picturesque landscaping in the closing years of the century.

In the 1770s, Johnes must have been frustrated by his own inability to take on a serious estate project. His chance came, however, following the death of his father. He soon decided, against the advice of family and friends, to leave Croft for Hafod. In a letter of 1783, he contrasts his free enthusiasm for Hafod ('This place is my own, and I trust when finished will realize my idea of ressembling a fairy scene') with the constraints he would have expected in remaining at Croft (' ... was I to cut down any trees which I certainly should do, to make walks etc., this would soon be misrepresented, and I a poor tenant at will should be served with an ejectment.').[10]

In 1794, Johnes wrote to George Cumberland thus: '.. I am anxious to shew you, who have seen this place in its original wildness, that by *beautifying it* I have *neither shorn* or *tormented* it.'[11] At first sight, the notion of 'beautifying' may appear to be at variance with the principles of Payne Knight and Price for whom 'roughness' was an aesthetic element to be emphasised in the context of the Picturesque. However, we may see 'beautifying' as part of the mature expression of theories initiated (and put into practice) earlier by the two Herefordshire squires.

For Johnes, the importance of roughness must have been a decisive element in his selecting Cardiganshire in preference to Croft for the expression of his own landscape ideal. At Hafod, Johnes' raw material was rich in the rough and wild, and relatively poor in the beautiful. By contrast, the Herefordshire raw material of Price and Payne Knight required 'roughening' rather than 'beautifying' if it were to accord with the Picturesque requirements of variety and contrast.

In considering picturesque landscapes of this period, it is important to note that roughness and wildness *per se* do not represent Picturesqueness - beauty and smoothness were essential too. However, it is not surprising that the rough and wild were emphasised by the English theorists since they were the ingredients which were in short supply in the lowland scenery of England. In Wales, and at Hafod in particular, there was a surfeit of wildness, requiring additions of beauty to achieve the balance and variety necessary to achieve the true Picturesque.

Johnes, as the last of the aforementioned trio to develop an extensive picturesque landscape, benefited from earlier attempts to realise the Picturesque on the ground. Furthermore, he is known to have acknowledged a debt to *The English Garden*, a poem containing didactic principles by William Mason, a close friend of William Gilpin.[12] Johnes developed an approach to landscaping which derived much from Payne Knight, based on the formation of a path of modest width which introduced the visitor into a sequence of contrasting scenes, developing in time and in space. In the history of the Picturesque, this approach may be seen as a translation of Gilpin's compositional theory of Picturesque observation (a static activity), into a thematic development of Picturesque experiences characterised in random sequence by beauty, roughness and sublimity. Because of the requirement for movement along a path, and the changing progression of 'pictures' thereby offered, this type of Picturesque design might reasonably be referred to as the 'progressive Picturesque'.[13]

At Downton, Foxley, and especially at Hafod, artefacts were few and far between. At Hafod, they were also exceedingly modest in scale. Thus, these 'progressive Picturesque' landscapes were different in concept from Hawkstone or Painshill, for example, where the scale and concentration (respectively) of the manifestations of constructed art were so much greater. Cumberland was impressed by the relatively unadorned character of Hafod, concluding his first chapter thus

'Yet one must be nice not to be content at first to visit the best points of view by the general routine; for all that is here done, has been to remove obstructions, reduce the materials, and conceal the art; and we are no where presented with attempts to force these untamed-streams, or indeed to invent any thing, where nature, the great mistress, has left all art behind; and where I find my favourite maxim has obtained to the extent of my wishes.

"Here nature feeds, the verdure points the views,
"While art, her handmaid, soberly pursues,
"Supports her sacred train, divides the groves,
"And, at due distance, with discretion moves." '

Clearly, it is the integrated whole of Hafod that captivated Cumberland by its naturalness - the 'general routine' of selective viewing from the best points would deny appreciation of the thematic progressions which Cumberland's text describes.

Johnes' progressive Picturesque may be seen as a major element in the complex reappraisal of the aesthetic of wildness which came to a head in the 1780s and 1790s. While conforming in many important ways with the didactic prescriptions of Payne Knight and Uvedale Price,[14] Johnes' picturesque landscape work extended the range of dynamic contrasts. Cumberland recorded reposeful beauty in the 'sweet, sheltered, level walk' of the 'warm, screened, and solitary retirement' of the riverside meadow. But, at Maen Arthur, beyond Pontrhydygroes, he encountered an opposing sublimity in the 'cold depth of the dark basons' and the 'violence of the flood' capable of eliciting such 'thrilling sensations of terror, which ever arise from majestical, yet gloomy exhibitions'. Cumberland's text leaves one in no doubt that Hafod was a place capable of provoking strong responses, a landscape to be felt as well as viewed, and that its walks extended the range of picturesque subjects in an unparalleled way.

Through its description, in aesthetic language, of the progression of scenes experienced from the walks, Cumberland's seminal *An Attempt to Describe Hafod* is crucial to our understanding of Johnes' unique interpretation of the Picturesque.

GEORGE CUMBERLAND

George Cumberland (1754-1848) was a polymath, who in 1784 was fortunate enough to inherit a comfortable annual income, enabling him to give up his job in an insurance office and devote himself to travelling extensively and pursuing an extraordinarily wide range of interests. He is best known for his membership of a circle comprising some of the most respected artists of the day, including William Blake, Thomas Stothard, and John Flaxman. Cumberland was both a patron and an active participant in the field of visual arts, being a collector, painter, engraver, and writer of art criticism and landscape appreciation. He also wrote poetry, and contributed articles and letters to journals on subjects as diverse as literature, agricultural theory and practice, social and political reform, and new developments in engineering - including numerous inventions of his own. In the latter half of his life. which he passed at Clifton, near Bristol, he became recognised through his research and publications as a distinguished geologist.[15]

Cumberland is known to have made at least four visits to Hafod, the first occurring in 1784, when he toured Wales on horseback in the company of Charles Long.[16] In his journal of the tour, Cumberland gives a most entertaining account of their adventures at the then little-known Devil's Bridge and makes a passing reference to Hafod, though at that time Thomas Johnes had scarcely begun the task of building his new mansion and 'beautifying' its grounds, and Cumberland was not yet personally acquainted with him. It appears that the two were introduced some ten years later, by Johnes' cousin, Richard Payne Knight; they went on to become loyal friends and regular correspondents.[17] Within a short time of their first meeting, Cumberland was receiving pressing invitations from Johnes to return and view the improvements made at Hafod. In 1795, Cumberland stayed as Johnes' guest for a period of two weeks, in the course of which he gathered the material for his book.

HAFOD IN 1795 AND 'BLAKE'S' MAP

Whilst there can be no question that the text of *An Attempt to Describe Hafod* was created from Cumberland's personal observations of the landscape, the origins of the accompanying engraved map are far less clear. It is assumed that the map was based on contemporary estate plans provided by Johnes, but now lost. Whatever its provenance, the map has become an invaluable historical source, confirming the existence and location of features for which little or no other evidence remains. Many of the farms and cottages shown pre-dated Johnes, but other features had been added to the landscape by him in the preceding ten years, including the 'new way to the House', the mansion itself, the Flower Garden, and the Cold Bath. Features such as Mariamne's Garden and the Bedford Monument, with which modern readers may be familiar, are absent from the map simply because they did not exist in 1795. A church is shown, but it is not the structure built for Johnes by James Wyatt (*ca.* 1800), but its predecessor, erected by the Herbert family in 1620. Finally, one should note the inclusion of one feature which seems never to have existed, namely the Druid Temple.

There is a widely-held belief that the map (which is unsigned) was engraved by Cumberland's friend and collaborator, William Blake, though no documentary evidence exists to link Blake to the map. The attribution is based on the unorthodox serifs attached to Blake's handwritten 'g's, and indeed these may be seen in the engraved text on the map. An alternative possibility is that the map was engraved by Cumberland himself, perhaps with lettering added by Blake. The picture is further complicated by the fact that, in 1795, Cumberland was receiving instruction from Blake in the techniques of engraving, and they both contributed illustrations to another of Cumberland's books, *Thoughts on Outline*, published in the same year as *An Attempt to Describe Hafod*. One must therefore keep an open mind and hope that future research may clarify the matter of the map's authorship.[18]

Jennifer Macve and Andrew Sclater

THE ARTIST THOMAS JONES AT HAFOD

In the autumn of 1786, Thomas Jones of Pencerrig visited Hafod and made a series of pencil sketches, each about 12.5 x 16 cm in size.[19]   Thomas Jones (1742-1803), the second son of a Radnorshire squire, had been a pupil of the great landscape painter Richard Wilson.[20] He became a professional artist whose main interest was in landscape, not simply the distant scene, but also its individual components - rocks, trees and buildings.

Jones' sketchbook of 1786 is devoted mainly to the picturesque landscapes of the valleys of the river Ystwyth at Hafod, and of the Rheidol around Devil's Bridge. In some forty sketches, Jones captured the essential features of both valleys in their most attractive parts. At Hafod, the artist revealed the natural amphitheatre which forms the topographical setting (Sketch 30), the visual excitement of paths winding through woods (6, 8), the contrast between open spaces and groves of trees (36*), the overlapping 'side-screens' of forested slopes (32) and the sinuous course of the Ystwyth in its valley (9*). A detailed account of these views has been published by the Friends of Hafod.[21]

Of special interest are the studies of ancient trees: gnarled, twisted, sometimes broken off, and often growing out of a steep bank, where they maintained a precarious

10

hold as soil was eroded from among their roots (15*, 19*, 21*, 31* and others). They are reminiscent of the 'arboreal furniture', which occurs so frequently in the foregrounds of grand classical landscape compositions. The more finished views followed the Wilsonian model, showing, for example, a tranquil scene of meadow, water, and wooded hillside framed by trees (30). Some views were lightly sketched, perhaps unfinished, or simply intended as rough notes.

The dated sketches suggest that Thomas Jones spent nine days at or near Hafod in September 1786 (10th to 18th), returning on the 3rd of October. All the trees appear to be deciduous and to be still in full leaf. The artist could produce meticulous detail, especially on the trunks of trees, but at times adopted a sweeping, simplified foliage reminiscent of the style of his fellow artist and friend, Francis Towne (12).

It is arguable whether even the most slender saplings visible in the sketches could have been planted by Thomas Johnes, who had inherited the estate only six years earlier. Most of the individual trees must have originated during the days of earlier occupiers, and it is more likely that they were self-sown than planted.[22] However, there would have been time for Johnes to make his mark on the scene by thinning.

Few man-made structures are shown in the sketches. Buildings appear in four instances: a stone cottage (14), two thatched buildings side by side (22), an arch (12), and a little crenellated tower on an eminence (40). The latter two could well be ornamental features, but whether built by Johnes it is impossible to say. Curiously, the artist made no attempt to show the existing house, or Thomas Baldwin's new creation, then under construction.

The bridge across the Ystwyth, just below the house, appears in two drawings (38*, 39). Known as the Alpine or Bwlchgwallter Bridge, it is shown as an outline 'T' suggesting a wooden framework resting on a central stone pier. The view is too distant to show details of construction, but it differs markedly from its replacement which appears in a later etching by J.G. Wood, dated 1812, which had two subtending arches.[23] The history and construction of this bridge attracted considerable research and discussion in the 1990s, when plans were drawn up for the reinstatement of a footbridge over the existing abutments. Jones also drew two bridges across the Rheidol: 'Pontpren plucca' (42) and 'Pont pren llwyd' (48), the latter with a water-mill nearby. Ironically, from the detail shown, it would be relatively simple to reconstruct either.

That other views of Hafod by Jones existed is confirmed by Benjamin Heath Malkin. Visiting the mansion in 1803, the topographical writer noted, above the doors of the winter dining room, 'four coloured drawings of scenes within the precincts of Havod' by Thomas Jones.[24] These may have been destroyed in the disastrous fire of 1807.

To put Jones' views of Hafod into context, some outline of his life is called for. Originally destined for the Church, he entered Jesus College, Oxford, in 1759, but left without taking a degree on account of the death of his great-uncle and benefactor. Turning to his boyhood predilection, he trained at Shipley's drawing school in London, and later became a pupil of Richard Wilson. He worked in Italy for seven years, frequenting a circle of British artists in Rome and acquiring new patrons among the gentlemen arriving from other parts of Europe on the Grand Tour.

Jones was both a prolific artist and an assiduous diarist. His early life is described in a detailed Journal, which he

12

distilled into *Memoirs*.[25] This vivid account of his daily life as an artist alludes to many of his own pictures and describes the circumstances of their production. In his own time, he did not achieve the fame his talents deserved, possibly being overshadowed by his master, Richard Wilson. Even today, recognition has been tardy. There is a representative collection of his pictures in the National Museum of Wales, and his work attracts fresh attention when shown in special exhibitions. He used oils, both on canvas and on paper, pencil, ink, wash and watercolour.

His home at Pencerrig, homes of friends and relatives in Wales and England, and his tours in Italy all provided subjects for his landscape work. Pencerrig lay in the undulating Radnorshire countryside a few miles south of Llandrindod Wells on the road to Builth. Jones successfully captured the characteristic rounded hills of his county in brush or pencil works, and was fascinated by its intimate hollows, rocks and hillocks and by the gnarled trunks of trees. He used such details for symbolic effect in his grander canvases. His history paintings, 'The Bard' (1774) and 'Shakespeare's Tempest; a Storm' (1777-8), both show shattered trees as signs of tension and disaster.

In Italy, Jones depicted views familiar to contemporary tourists and still popular today - Tivoli, Ariccia, Vesuvius, Lake Nemi, the Bay of Naples and the grottoes of Posillipo. He painted the scene of some early archaeological discoveries - 'An Excavation of an Antique Building Discovered in a Cava in the Villa Negroni at Rome' (1777). In Naples, he painted views composed entirely of buildings, showing their square shapes at close quarters with a realism that has a strikingly modern appeal.[26]

He returned from Italy in 1783 to settle in London, but a paucity of commissions led him to fear for his career.

However, his financial anxieties must have been eased by the inheritance of a small landed estate from his father, who died at Pencerrig in December 1782. Contrary to his expectations of an untrammelled artistic life, the entire family estate passed to Thomas after the death of his elder brother, Major John Jones, in 1787. He left London for Pencerrig with his wife and two daughters in 1789, and took up the life of a country squire. He participated in the social life of the county, and was appointed High Sheriff of Radnorshire in 1791. He died in 1803 and was buried in Llandrindod Wells, at Caebach Chapel, which had been founded by his great-uncle, Thomas Jones of Trefonnen.[27].

Thomas Jones had stopped writing his Journal three years before making his drawings of Hafod, so we cannot look to the Journal for more information; in a short Appendix dealing with his later years, he made no reference to Hafod. We have, therefore, to rely for evidence on the views themselves. They demonstrate his artistic taste and familiarity with the conventions of landscape composition, and they also prove that he could observe and record reality with skill and accuracy. The Hafod drawings form a substantial and reliable addition to the pictorial evidence for the appearance of the landscape early in the occupancy of Thomas Johnes, and they complement the prose of George Cumberland's *An Attempt to Describe Hafod.*

Donald Moore

[1] William Gilpin, *Observations on the River Wye*. 2nd edition. London: R. Blamire, 1789, p.78.

[2] Stephen Daniels and Charles Watkins (eds.) *The Picturesque Landscape: Visions of Georgian Herefordshire*. Nottingham: Dept. of Geography, University of Nottingham, 1994, p.64, fig. 7.

[3] For an appreciation of Devil's Bridge and its place in Picturesque tourism, see Jennie Macve, 'The Picturesque Response to Devil's Bridge' in *Welsh Historic Gardens Trust Newsletter*, No. 8, 1995, pp. 3-12.

[4] The two principal sources for contemporary theory are Richard Payne Knight, *The Landscape: a didactic poem*. London, 1794, and Uvedale Price, *An Essay on the Picturesque*. London, 1794. Daniels and Watkins *op. cit.* provides a good introduction to the major influence of Knight and Price on picturesque practice in Herefordshire estates in the late eighteenth century.

[5] For an appraisal of the significance of Gilpin, see C.P. Barbier, *William Gilpin: His Drawings, Teachings and Theory of the Picturesque*. Oxford: Clarendon Press, 1963.

[6] A photographic example of the Claude Glass is given in Malcolm Andrews, *The Search for the Picturesque: Landscape Aesthetics and Tourism in Britain, 1760-1800*. Aldershot: Scolar Press, 1989, p.68, fig. 12.

[7] Michael Symes, *William Gilpin at Painshill*. Painshill Park Trust, 1995. An excellent summary of Gilpin's ideas.

[8] Richard J. Moore-Colyer, *A Land of Pure Delight: Selections from the letters of Thomas Johnes of Hafod, 1748-1816*. Llandysul: Gomer Press, 1992.. The introduction provides a succinct account of Johnes' life, social circle and interests.

[9] David Whitehead, 'Sense with Sensibility: Landscaping in Georgian Herefordshire' in Daniels and Watkins, *op. cit.*, pp.16-33.

[10] Moore-Colyer, *op. cit.*, pp.86-87.

[11] Moore-Colyer, *op. cit.*, p.101.

[12] Mavis Batey, 'The English Garden in Welsh' in *Garden History*, Vol.22, No.2, 1994, pp.157-161.

[13] Andrew Sclater, 'Sublime Irregularities and the Design of Hafod. 1. Thomas Johnes' First Walk' in *The Picturesque*, No. 8, 1994, pp.16-23.

[14] see 4 above.

[15] G.E. Bentley, Jr., *A Bibliography of George Cumberland*. New York/London: Garland Publishing, 1975; James King, *William Blake*. London: Weidenfeld and Nicolson, 1991.

[16] George Cumberland, *Journal of a tour in Wales*. Microfilm No. 215, National Library of Wales. Records a tour made in 1784 with Charles Long (1760-1838), to whom *An Attempt to Describe Hafod* is dedicated. Long laid out an estate which was the subject of Cumberland's only other published description of a country estate: *Bromley Hill, The Seat of the Rt. Hon. Charles Long, M.P. A Sketch.*, London: T. Bentley and Son, 1816.

[17] For a selection of Johnes' letters to Cumberland, see Moore-Colyer, *op. cit.*

[18] G.E. Bentley, Jr., *Blake Books*, Oxford: Clarendon Press, 1977, pp.540-541; *Idem.*, *Blake Books Supplement*, Oxford: Clarendon Press, 1995, pp.204-206; Jack Lindsay, *William Blake: his Life and Work*. London: Constable, 1978.

[19] Thomas Jones numbered his sketches. References to sketches in the introduction are by number. An asterisk indicates that a given sketch is reproduced in this publication.

[20] Prys Morgan, 'Thomas Jones of Pencerrig' in *Trans. Hon. Soc. Cymmrodorion*, 1984, pp.51-76.

[21] Roger Hallett, 'The "Hafod" Sketchbook of Thomas Jones' in *Friends of Hafod Newsletter,* No.5, 1991, pp.4-11.

[22] Andrew Sclater, *Hafod Conservation Strategic Plan*. Report for Welsh Historic Gardens Trust, 1991, pp.26-30.

[23] John George Wood, *The Principal Rivers of Wales*. London: T. Bensley, 1813.

[24] Benjamin Heath Malkin, *The Scenery, Antiquities ,and Biography of South Wales*. London: Longman and Rees, 1804.

[25] 'Memoirs of Thomas Jones' with an introduction by Paul Oppé, *The Walpole Society*, Vol.32, 1946-1948.

[26] Francis W. Hawcroft, *Travels in Italy 1776-1783, based on the Memoirs of Thomas Jones*. Exhibition catalogue, Manchester: Whitworth Art Gallery, 1988.

[27] R.C.B. Oliver, *The Family History of Thomas Jones the Artist of Pencerrig, Radnorshire..* Llandrindod Wells: privately published, 1987.

THE HAFOD TRUST

In 1991, the Welsh Historic Gardens Trust commissioned a report on Hafod entitled *Hafod Conservation Strategic Plan*. Ymddiriedolaeth yr Hafod/Hafod Trust, a charitable company, was formed in 1994 to continue the conservation and restoration work begun in 1993 by the Welsh Historic Gardens Trust, in partnership with the owners of the estate, Forest Enterprise (Forestry Commission). It is supported by both public and private funding.

The central theme of the partnership project is to revive (as far as possible) the landscape experience prevailing in the time of Thomas Johnes, by restoring the circuit walks described by Cumberland in 1796. *An Attempt to Describe Hafod* is the most important single source informing the Trust's work.

At the time of writing, restoration of the First (or Lady's) Walk is well advanced, and work on the Second (or Gentleman's) and New Walks is planned. Reconstruction of the collapsed Alpine Bridge across the River Ystwyth, linking the First and Second Walks, has just been completed. Masonry of various dates has been carefully repaired, and the design of the superstructure is based upon that of the last bridge to occupy the site.

AN ATTEMPT TO DESCRIBE

HAFOD, *&c.*

AN ATTEMPT TO DESCRIBE

HAFOD,

AND THE NEIGHBOURING SCENES ABOUT THE
BRIDGE OVER THE FUNACK, COMMONLY CALL-
ED THE DEVIL's BRIDGE, IN THE COUNTY OF
CARDIGAN.

AN ANCIENT SEAT BELONGING TO THOMAS
JOHNES, ESQ. MEMBER FOR THE COUNTY OF
RADNOR.

BY GEORGE CUMBERLAND.

Unvex'd with quarrels, undisturb'd with noise,
The country king his peaceful realm enjoys;
Cool grots, and living lakes, the flow'ry pride
Of meads, and streams that thro' the valley glide,
And shady groves, that easy sleep invite,
And, after toilsome days, a soft repose at night.

Dryden's Virgil.

LONDON:
Printed by W. Wilson, St. Peter's Hill, Doctors' Commons.
And sold by T. Egerton, Whitehall.

M DCC XCVI.

TO

CHARLES LONG, Esq. M. P.

—

WHEN, traverſing the Cambrian mountains, in the eager purſuit of picturesque beauty, we once united in opinion, that, among all the wonders of Welch ſcenery, none had any title to be compared to HAFOD, *and the ſurrounding country; neither of us then, I believe, expected to ſee a little palace ariſe among thoſe receſſes, or that the merit of thoſe ſublime irregularities of nature would ſo ſoon find a taſteful owner to appreciate their magnificence.*

a 2   *Much*

Much lefs did we then anticipate a meeting in SWITZERLAND, *where, after a tour through the moft romantic parts of that country, we fhould again agree, that* HAFOD *and the* FALL *of* PEN-MACKNA *ftill flourifhed unrivalled; and that our native land poffeffed charms, which, in defpite of climate, at certain feafons, ftood prominent among the objects moft worthy of delineation.*

At my laft return from the Continent, the fame fentiment induced me to print a few copies of the little Poem on Britifh Landfcapes; in which, by the following note, I, in a manner, pledged myfelf to revifit a fpot, that had made, on my mind, fo diftinct an impreffion.

In that note, I faid, (CLIFDEN *gives a fine fpecimen of the magnificent ftile of nature at* PIERCFIELD; *but with all its beauties, to thofe who have vifited the latter, it feems only a fragment torn from the fides of that majeftic work; and yet, between* CLIFDEN *and* PIERCFIELD,

there

there is nothing approaching it in grandeur. The country, about the DEVIL'S BRIDGE *and* HA- VOD, *furpaffes either ; containing fcenery fo fu- premely beautiful, that the author, having paffed a few days there making drawings, meditated the defign of compofing a defcription to accompany them ; but too much enchanted to give it with coolnefs, he relinquifhed the contemplation ; and all he can now fay is, that having, fince that time, vifited all the fine fcenes of* SWITZERLAND, SAVOY, *the* TYROL, *and* ITALY, *truth compels him to give many parts of* WALES *the preference, except the advantages derived from clearer fkies ; and a cir- cumflance that fhould give this teftimony additional weight is, that fatiated with landfcape, fince his acquaintance with the highefl efforts of human art, the fculpture of the ancients, his before heated imagination is cooled fufficiently to fee the face of nature with difcriminate delight).*

In the autumn of 1794, *I had ocular demonftra- tion of the propriety of this note, and the juftice of thofe remarks ; for, after a moft attentive exami-*

nation

nation of these remarkable regions, I returned
through our fine English scenes, as through a
barren plain, uninterested; and with my faculties
impressed with so warm an attachment to that romantic country, as still to retain its attraction,
though constantly resident on one of the most pleasing
and salubrious situations near the metropolis. Nor
let it be considered as a trivial proof of the influence
of fine nature over us, that, without consulting our
friend, I cannot resist the temptation I feel to un-
veil his Elysium, and to call on your well-known
taste to support the genuine approbation.

BISHOPSGATE,
WINDSOR GREAT PARK,
JANUARY I, 1796.

G. C.

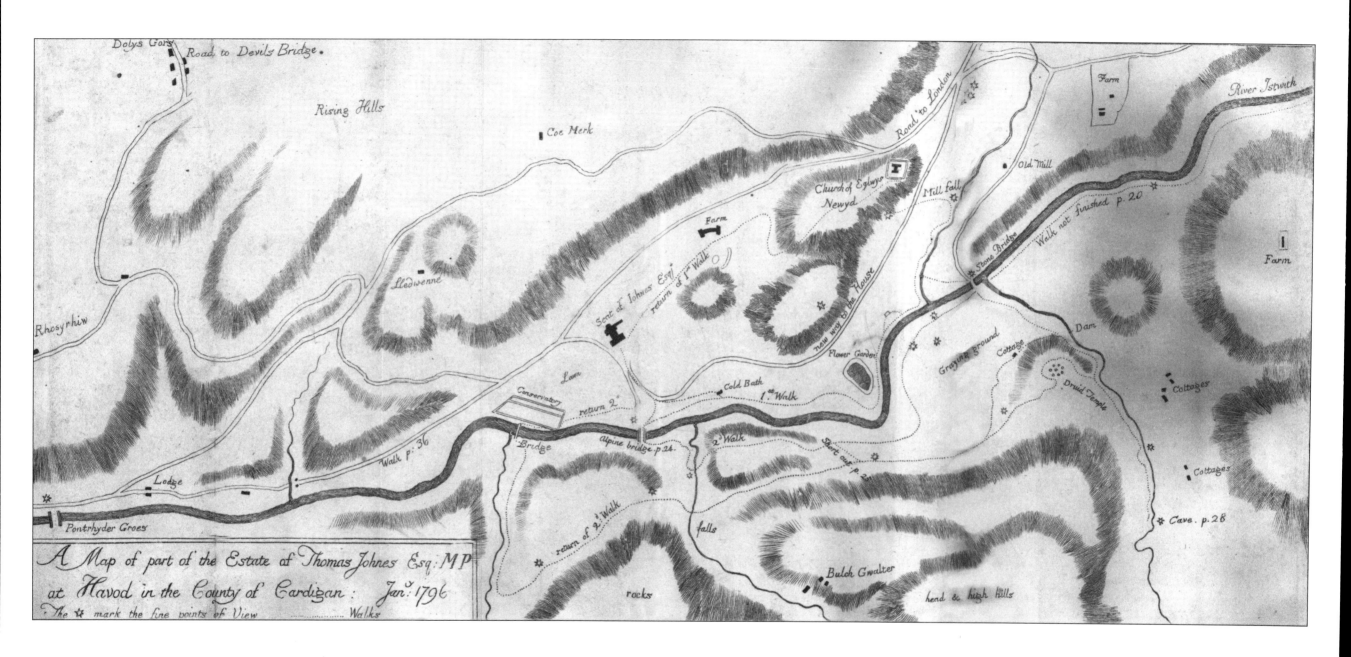

Dolys Gors

Road to Devils Bridge.

Rising Hills

Coe Merk

Road to London

Farm

River Istwith

Church of Eglwys Newyd

Old Mill

Mill fall

Farm

Lledwenne

Farm

Walk not finished p. 20

Seat of Johnes Esq.

return of 1.ᵗ Walk

Stone Bridge

new way to the House

Rhosyrhiw

Dam

Flower Garden

Grazing ground

Cottage

Lawn

Cold Bath

Druid Temple

Conservatory

1.ˢᵗ Walk

Cottages

return 2.ᵈ

Walk p. 36

Bridge

Alpine bridge p. 24.

2.ᵈ Walk

Short cut p. 22

Lodge

return of 2.ᵈ Walk

falls

Cave. p. 28

Pontrhyder Groes

rocks

Bulch Gwalter

head & high hills

A Map of part of the Estate of Thomas Johnes Esq.ʳ MP
at Havod in the County of Cardigan: Jan.ʳ 1796

The ✧ mark the fine points of View .... Walks

HAFOD.

" Come. bleffed Pan, whom rural haunts delight;
" Come, leaping, agile, wand'ring, ftarry light;
" Thee fhepherds, ftreams of water, goats' rejoice
" Thou lov'ft the chace, and echo's fecret voice,
" Come, Bacchanalian, bleffed pow'r, draw near."

Taylor's 10*th Hymn of Orpheus.*

Hafod, ufually pronounced Havod, is a place in itfelf fo pre-eminently beautiful, that it highly merits a particular defcription. It ftands furrounded with fo many noble fcenes, diverfified with elegance as well as with grandeur; the country on the approach to it is fo very wild and uncommon, and the place itfelf is now fo embellifhed by art, that it will be difficult, I believe, to point out a fpot that can be put in competition with it, confidered either as the objeƈt of the Painter's Eye, the Poet's Mind, or as

A   a de-

a defirable refidence for thofe who, admirers
of the beautiful wildnefs of nature, love alfo
to inhale the pure air of afpiring mountains,
and enjoy that *fanto pacé* (as the Italians expref-
fively term it) which arifes from folitudes made
focial by a family-circle.

HAFOD, to all thefe charms, unites induce-
ments which, though not uncommon in England, have there, at fuch a diftance from the
capital, a peculiar grace. It has a capacious
ftone-manfion, executed in the pleafing, becaufe
appropriate ftile of Gothic architecture; fituated on the fide of a chofen, fheltered dingle,
embowered with trees, which rife from a lawn
of the gentleft declivity, that fhelves in graceful hollows to the ftream below.

From the portico it commands a woody,
narrow, winding vale; the undulating forms of
whofe afcending, fhaggy fides, are richly clothed
with various foliage, broken with filvery water-
falls, and crowned with climbing fheep-walks,
reaching to the clouds.

Neither are the luxuries of life abfent; for,
on the margin of the Yftwyth, where it flows
broadeft through this delicious vale, we fee hot
houfes

Hafod Octob'r 3d
1786

houfes, and a confervatory; beneath the rocks a bath; amid the receffes of the woods a flower-garden; and within the building, whofe decorations, though rich, are pure and fimple, we find a mafs of rare and valuable literature, whofe pages here feem doubly precious, where meditation finds fcope to range unmolefted.

In a word, fo many are the delights afforded by the fcenery of this place and its vicinity, to a mind imbued with any tafte, that the impreffion on mine was encreafed after an interval of ten years from the firft vifit, employed chiefly in travelling among the Alps, the Apennines, the Sabine Hills, the Tyrollefe; along the fhores of the Adriatic, over the Glaciers of Switzerland, and up the Rhine; where, though in fearch of beauty, I never, I feel, faw any thing fo fine, never fo many pictures concentered in one fpot; fo that, warmed by the renewal of my acquaintance with them, I am irrefiftibly urged to attempt a defcription of the hitherto almoft virgin-haunts of thefe obfcure mountains.

Wales, and its borders, both north and fouth, abound, at intervals, with fine things; Piersfield has grounds of great magnificence, and wonderfully picturefque beauty.

A 2   Downton.

4

Downton-Caftle * has a delicious woody
vale, moft taftefully managed; Llangollen is
brilliant; the banks of the *Conway* † favagely
grand; Barmouth romantically rural; the great
Piftill Rhayder is horribly wild; Rhyader Wen-
nol, gay, and glorioufly irregular; each of which
merits a ftudied defcription.

But, at HAVOD and its neighbourhood, I

---

* Downton Caftle, near Ludlow, is the feat of
Richard Paine Knight, Efq. member for that place;
and author of " A Poem on Landfcape." He has
laid out the valley (where Milton is faid to have
planned his Comus) in a ftile that does infinite
credit to his refined tafte; which has led him like-
wife to make one of the pureft and largeft collections
of good antique bronze-fculpture in Europe, after the
mufeum at Portici, and which is really a valuable
acquifition to this country.

† " ———— Conway crown'd with wood,
" And rocks encompafs'd round, augments the flood.
" Forth from the giant-hills fhe takes her way,
" Refiftlefs winds, and moves with fov'reign fway;
" With flow, majeftic fweep, creates her bed,
" Wide, and more wide, the pregnant waters fpread;
" While herds, from purple hills, look down below,
" And rocks inverted on her furface glow."

find

find the effects of all in one circle ; united with
this peculiarity, that the deep dingles, and
mighty woody flopes, which, from a different
fource, conduct the Rhydols' never-failing waters from Plenlimmon, and the Fynach, are of a
unique character, as mountainous forefts, accompanying gigantic fize with graceful forms ;
and, taking altogether, I fee the " Sweeteft
" interchange of hill and valley, rivers, woods,
" and plains, and falls with foreft crown'd,
" rocks, dens, and caves ;" infomuch, that it
requires little enthufiafm there to feel forcibly
with Milton, that

" All things that be, fend up from earth's great altar,
" Silent praife."———

To the judicious traveller, who is defirous, in
his tour, to afcend in a regular fcale of fine places,
let it be ever recommended, if, in his paffage
to this place, he come from the metropolis, to
begin with the village of Tintern, near Chep-
ftow, which, though little noticed, even by
thofe * who magnify the pretty landfcapes near

---

* If Mr. Gilpin, who has made a chaos of art,
as far as the fubject he treats of is connected with it,
had

the Wye, is yet abundantly picturefque and
rural; and where an artift, poffeffed of the rare
talent of knowing how to chufe, might foon fill
his portfolio.

He fhould next devote three or four days, at
leaft, to Piersfield, and then afcend the Wye
from Monmouth, up as far as Hereford; next
follow it by Builth, and the Hay, to Rhayader-
Gwy-bridge, taking the Falls of the *Ithon* on
the way; thence paffing by the picturefque lake
and torrent of Gwynllyn, which is about two
miles from Rhayader-Gwy-bridge, it is eafy, by
turning a little over to the right, to regain the
high road to *Hafod* and Aberyftwyth. On entering thefe mountains, like the prelude to fome

---

had poffeffed this talent, he would not have had oc-
cafion to lament the want of fore-grounds, and to
advife practitioners to invent them *ad libitum:*—
even a bright ftubble field is often the beft fore-ground
for the picture; for it frequently occafions us, by
its fimplicity and plainnefs, to obferve the grandeur
of the fcene beyond; and, in the hands of a genuine
artift, may be fo managed, as to give a value to the
whole: for effect is not dependent on ftrong maffes
of fhade, but on fharpnefs or bluntnefs of outline.

fcene

scene of enchantment, we are prefented with a
contraft that is really awful; our winding road
hanging on the precipitous fides of fteep, fmooth,
and mighty hills, cloathed to their very tops
with verdure, befpotted all over with numerous
flocks, and herds of black cattle, vaguely grazing the tender grafs, or picking a fcanty fufte-
nance near the pendant brow of fome po-
lifhed hillock ; and this at a giddy height that
makes one dread, left the unfure ground fhould
flide beneath their feet, and fend them down, a
living ruin, to the deeps below ; for, from the
haughty fides of thefe hanging lawns, down to
the water-worn fmooth, dark rock, that forms
the torrent's bed, not a fhrub, or fuzzy protu-
berance, appears to break their fall.

As to the river, that rolls at the feet of thefe
graffy mountains, the channel is fo fudden, and
fo deep, that, even from the towering road on
the fide of this valley, one can only by con-
jecture imagine, that far down its waters

" Creep in lingering lab'rinths dark and flow."

Such are the reflections naturally arifing in the
mind of an Englifh traveller, when occafionally
the

the fingularity of the fcene forces him, for a moment, to turn his eyes from the fearful road he
is defcending, to furvey the majeftic picture
which lies around.

Yet oftentimes he finds himfelf on a level
plain, with a turbary, or bog, extending to the
foot of the hills ; whofe dark and yawning fiffures ftrongly recal Milton's wonderful picture
of one, in thefe lines :

" ———— Quench'd in a boggy fyrtis, neither fea
" Nor good dry land, nigh founder'd, on he fares,
" Treading the crude confiftence."

Thus thefe moory dales, thefe gloomy crags
thefe rocks with frowning brows, enhance the
value of even the rugged road that leads through
them ; and, continuing thefe fcenes for fome
miles, with little variety, except now and then
the ftorm-beaten abode of fome laborious fhep-
herd, we come at laft to a modern bridge, and
find our way lies under fteep precipices, on the
right of the valley, near fome old mines of lead-
ore ; whofe dingy fcrofa, impending above the
high road, choaks the river into which it falls,
and which now runs broad and fhallow through
the vale, manifefting to the admiring fpectator the
amplitude of the excavations into the bowels of
the

the rock, whilst the powder-blasted, gloomy crags, that scowl above the aperture, convey no bad idea of the sulphurous soil of Milton's nether world.

Within the mines there are said to be abundance of chambers, but the workmen sleep in cottages abroad; and these, united with the engine-wheel, banish considerably the natural gloom of the place, which, being divested of trees, and scanty indeed of cultivation, reminds a lover of *Cervantes* not unfrequently of the sable mountains, where the love-stricken, veteran knight listened to

" Stunning founds, borne thro' the hollow dark."
Milton.

Just beyond the mines, their present tenant has built an inn; where, although the delicate can find no comfortable accommodation, suited even to common ideas of enjoyment, yet a zealous admirer of the fine scenes, that now begin to unfold themselves, must, alas! take up his lodging; for, in all these parts, no other resting-place occurs, except a little public cottage,*

---

* This is now, I am informed, very considerably enlarged, and made a comfortable in, where travellers may be well accommodated.

built

built by the hofpitable proprietor of HAFOD,
and the Devil's Bridge, on the very brow of a
fteep, woody hill, above the *Fynach*-Fall, front-
ing fcenes of ftupendous magnificence.

As to Spitty-Cenfen, where, over the door
of a cavern, we fee infcribed,

" Go north, go fouth, go eaft, go weft,
" When paft this, you've paft the beft."

The horrors of that abode of mifery are a
compleat contraft to the grandeur of the fcenes
around it.

The crifped heads of Hafod's woods now
burft all at once on the aftonifhed eye.

To the right, the road to Aberyftwith, afcends
the verdant hills ; below them, the little church
of Eglwys Newydd prefents its modeft front,
half buried in oaks, feated on a little knoll ; in
front, the woody valley, with the Yftwyth, in
its bottom, opens before us, crowned on the left
with floping, lofty hills ; while, in the midft, a
fmooth mound, half concealed with oaks, rifes
among the fhades, and feems defigned by nature
as a centre ; whence, nor too high, nor too low,
the whole expanfe around, of intermingled
beauties, may continually feed the eye : where,
if

if a druid's temple never ftood, a druid's temple
is unqueftionably called for; and, I cannot help
expreffing a hope, that a rude imitation will
one day theie be placed *.

Defcending by a left-hand entrance-road,
among a grove of oaks, you wind under the
knoll, that fuftains the little church; and, foon
turning to the right, come fuddenly and unex-
pectedly on the Gothic manfion, facing the portico front; which, with its light wings, white,
gay appearance, and fpacious fteps, feems to
invite its vifitors with cheerful hofpitality.

There are four fine walks from the houfe,
chiefly through ways artificially made by the
proprietor; all dry, kept clean, and compofed
of materials found on the fpot; which is chiefly
a coarfe ftone, of a grayifh caft, friable in
many places, and like flate, but oftener confift-
ing of immenfe maffes, that coft the miner, in
making fome part of thefe walks, exceffive la-
bour; for there are places, where it was neceffary to perforate the rock many yards, in order
to pafs a promontory, that, jutting acrofs the
way, denied further accefs; and to go round

---

* Such I find fince is the intention of Mr. Johnes.

which

which, you muft have taken a great tour, and
made a fatiguing defcent. As it is, the walks
are fo conducted, that few are fteep ; the tranfi-
tions eafy, the returns commodious, and the
branches diftinct. Neither are they too many,
for much is left for future projectors ; and if a
man be ftout enough to range the underwoods,
and faftidious enough to reject all trodden paths,
he may, almoft every where, ftroll from the
ftudied line, till he be glad to regain the friendly
conduct of the well-known way.

Yet one muft be nice not to be content at firft
to vifit the beft points of view by the general
routine ; for all that is here done, has been to
remove obftructions, reduce the materials, and
conceal the art; and we are no where prefented
with attempts to force thefe untamed-ftreams, or
indeed to invent any thing, where nature, the
great miftrefs, has left all art behind ; and where
I find my favourite maxim has obtained to the
extent of my wifhes.

" Here nature feeds, the verdure points the views,
" While art, her handmaid, foberly purfues,
" Supports her facred train, divides the groves,
" And, at due diftance, with difcretion moves."

Poem on Britifh Landfcape.

at Hafod
Cardiganshire
16 Sept. 1786

" —— Unto the woode that was me faſt by,
" I went forthe myſelf alone boldily,
" And helde the way down by a broke ſide,
" Tyll I came to a launde of white and greene,
" So fair an one had I never in bene;
" The grounde was greene y' powdir'd with daiſye,
" The flouris and the grevis alike hie,
" All grene and white, was nothing ellis ſene.

CHAUCER.

THE firſt ramble I ſhould chuſe for a ſtranger would be, to take him down, through the lawn before the houſe, at once to the river Yſtwith; where, inſtead of paſſing over the long Alpine bridge, one turns ſhort to the left into a path that ſkirts the water, and beneath which it runs rapidly over its pebbly bed, overhung with ſtraggling boughs.

Thence you ſoon deſcend to the level of the mead, through which it flows; where, after
paſſing

(14)

paffing the cold bath, that is fed by a conftant
fpring of the pureft water,

" Where from the rock, with liquid lapfe diftills
" A limpid fount."———

Pope's Odyffey, book xvii. *line* 232.

" The watre is evir frefh and newe,
" That welmith up, with waves bright,
" The mountenaunce of two finger height,
" About it is the graffe fpringing."

Chaucer's Romant. of the Rofe, line 1560.

you enter a fweet, fheltered, level walk, run-
ning nearly on a line with the river, but fepa-
rated from it by narrow and irregular ftripes of
meadow, and fhaded above by climbing woods,
and rocks fringed with old roots, and ivy.

This meadow, which feems to be quite hem-
med in by the woody hills, conveys an idea of
a warm, fcreened, and folitary retirement; at
the end of it, however, you are agreeably furprifed with a fudden turn of the ftream into a
confined valley; to the left of which lies, cap-
ped in high trees, a moft fequeftered fwell of
about two acres, formed into a flower and fhrub-
garden; furrounded by a rude ftone-fence, of
an irregular form, nearly concealed by ivy; the

plats

plats of which are curved out of a fine fhaven turf, and the whole circumfcribed by a fmooth gravel walk.

The fituation of this gay little fpot, among rocks and torrents, and backed by the nobleft woods, affords us, at our entrance, an agreeable furprife ; for, although clofe to the paths, unlefs fhown by the guide, it would not be difcovered ; fuddenly, however, you find yourfelf

" Among thick woven arborets, and flowers
" Embroider'd on each bank *."

Milton.

Iffuing from this quiet fcene, you arrive at the borders of a rapid torrent, that falls fpeedily

---

* " ———— Violaria et
" Myrtus, et omnis copia narium,
" Spargent olivetis odorem,
" Fertilibus domino priori."

Hor. ode xv. *lib.* 2.

" The violet and the myrtle greets
" The fenfes with a wafte of fweets!
" While vainly would Apollo's ray
" Through our thick laurels pour the day."

Francis.

into

into the Yftwyth, and the mouth of which
forms the pretty cafcade. The way now becomes rocky, and, afcending among groves, one's
attention is prefently arrefted by a picturefque
break of the water, juft by a rude ftone-bridge,
leaving which uncroffed, and continuing up this
mill-ftream, a number of pleafing falls murmur
all the way.

We now crofs over a fimple foot-bridge, that
embraces two rocks, and a few irregular paces
introduce you to another pafs; where the wave
foams loudly under the foundation of a ruftic
building, connected to the path by a wall; on
afcending a few fteps to this building, all is loft
by the fcreen it affords; but, on iffuing from it,
pleafure and furprize affect the mind delightfully, at the picture that ftarts as it were to
view—For now,

At a few hundred feet from you, the valley
feems to terminate in a moft romantic ftile,
ending with a fciffure in the rocky front; through
which is poured the whole ftream of the torrent,
tumbling from a pretty confiderable height, in
a form the moft agreeable, fcreened by a huge
mafs of bare rock, over which, in great floods,
it makes its courfe entire; but, in general, as
when

when I faw it, the waters wind behind the
rock; and, rufhing into a boiling pool, come
rattling forward, white with foam, and drop the
whole brook near the building, whence this
cafcade * is moft advantageoufly beheld.

If, after viewing it, you chufe to afcend the
fides of this old fall, you will meet with many
interefting details; and, although the way be a
little rugged, and the ftones flippery, I found
it amply recompence my curiofity.

Here, although we feem to come to the end
of our walk, it takes another turn, fhort to the
left; afcending, for this high country, through
very fine oak groves; for it is not at this place,
as in rich plains, that oaks are found of great
magnitude: here they derive their beauty chiefly from their forms and fituations, growing
generally from old ftocks; it having been the
cuftom of this country, for many years back,
to mow their woods, as it were, at ftated pe-
riods: much mercy has however been extended

---

* I had, one very dark night, the pleafure to fee
it lighted up by the Bengal-fire; and the effeft was
original and pleafing.

B   to

to the Dryades at Hafod ; and one feels a pleafing hope, that thefe forefts are now deftined to a
long repofe.

Afcending through thefe groves, among the
underwoods of which the fheep culls at random
her ivy, and flowery herbage ; you lofe fight, almoft entirely, of the torrent ; except where, at
a few intervals, little fpots of its white froth
glitter through the trees : But you never lofe the
found of the wave, which afcends with you, till
you arrive at a broader and more level walk, that
conveys you, ftill mounting flowly, into one of
the principal approach-ways, conducted through
clofe woods on the fides of a hill : on iffuing
through which, at a common gate, it continues
up, fecured on the fteep fide by a fence, and
prefently leads to an open, elevated fituation ;
whence almoft the whole valley is difcerned,
backed by fine forms of mountains, fome bare,
fome wooded.

At this point, I mean a few paces from the
common gate, that fine fmooth hill, mentioned
before as inviting a Druid's temple, appears in
a particularly interefting form ; feeming, by its
regular features, there to be placed as a happy
contraft to the furrounding theatre of wildnefs.

After

at Hafod Cardiganshire
18 Sep.r 1786

After afcending gently a little further, a returning path brings us to the church of Eglwys-
Newydd, niched in a wood, overgrown with
brambles,

> There nightingales in unprun'd copfes build,
> In fhaggy furzes lies the hare conceal'd.
> *Savage's Wanderer, canto* v.

among which the cattle have worn a thoufand
irregular paths, with its decent church-yard and
ancient yews about it ; while above, the climbing fheep-walks crown the paftoral landfcape.

For change the fmall church into a Temple
of Pan, and you have the very place where
the Comates of Theocritus fays

> ————— Τηνεὶ δρύες ὧδε κύπειρος,
> Ὡδε καλὸν βομβεῦντι ποτὶ σμάνισσι μέλισσαι.

Here reft we ; low Cyprus decks the ground,
Oaks lend their fhade, and wild bees buz around.
Fawkes.

Entering the brufhwood, a rural path-way
now carries you fpeedily to a very delightful
little promontory, rather clear of wood ; whence,
with a gentle precipice below, you command
the crefcent-formed farm-yard, crouching under

B 2 the

the hill, below the river, the bridge, and all
around the variegated vale.

This walk will take a full hour: there is another, in the fame direction, which branches
from it, fit only for thofe who can climb,
as it is not yet entirely traced; but which,
on that very account, may have inducement for
the curious.—To find this, you muft crofs the
rude ftone-bridge, before-mentioned as being
fituated juft beyond the flower-garden ; whence
a path foon leads to another ftone-bridge of
one arch, buttreffed by two folid rocks; beneath which, at a pretty confiderable depth, the
Yftwyth (here confined and girt in) pours its
whole ftream into a bafon, quite overfhadowed
with boughs of oaks.

Looking up the river, on the other fide of
this rude bridge, the water rolling heavily down
over vaft ftones, which often feparate the ftream,
has a very wild appearance : and a pretty confiderable mill-ftream, rufhing over the high
rocky bank, juft above the arch of the bridge,
forms a brawling cataract, not very large, but
extremely impetuous.

On

On the left, lofty wooded rocks afcend high over the river: on the right-hand, broken ground, covered with herbage, and loofe ftones, mark the irregular boundaries; and, on this fide, you muft afcend the confined ftream, which may eafily be effected, though the oppofite bank is too fteep to admit a path.

After fkirting the torrent's rocky bed, at in- tervals, for about half a mile upwards, a pretty little floping, cultivated fpot, on the oppofite fide, prefents itfelf before the eye; fufpended as it were over the ftream, and capt with a cottage; below which the water works a wind: after viewing this fpot, we fhould defcend to the point where the whole Yftwyth is feen, pour- ing through one of the nobleft maffes of rock that can be imagined, worn, by the winters' floods, into a pleafingly irregular form; fringed and fhaded with young oak and birch; and ter- minated above with a ftripe of floping meadow, which melts into the gentle declivities of a mountainous fheep-walk.

Upwards, the river again fpreads and widens; and through a rude grove is foon perceived a ftone-water-mill; whence, a long bridge, of two trees thrown acrofs the fhallow, rapid ftream,

B 3   invites

invites the paffage : inftead of which, continue
on the right-hand fide, till you meet a little
brook, fuch as one could almoft jump over ; on
following which to the right, under a fteep,
woody cliff, that clothes a fmall dingle, one
comes to a fweetly formed cafcade, which rolls
down from a confiderable height, over a fine
broken table of flaty rock ; and, fpreading itfelf like a fan, glides gently into the little
brook below.

" Part thou haſt view'd—if further we explore,
" Let *induſtry* deſerve applauſe the more;
" He clear'd, manur'd, enlarg'd the furtive ground,
" And firms the conqueſt with his fenceful mound;
" What wonder then *art* by his potent aid,
" A manſion in a barren mountain made."

Savage's Wanderer, canto i.

There are walks of great extent, on the oppoſite ſide the river from the houſe, which take
up about three hours to trace, returning again
to the manſion, and theſe are what are con-
ſidered as the principal part of the artificial im-
proved paths.

Whether they might have been better laid
out, I ſhall not attempt here to enquire ; for
indeed I was too much delighted with the accommodation they afforded me, to think much
of criticiſing their lines, if I had been poſſeſſed
of the requiſite abilities; I ſhall therefore content myſelf with deſcribing them, and the principal points of view they afford, whilſt their

delightful

delightful remembrance is freſh in my mind ; and from notes made on the ſpot.

Leaving the houſe, you muſt deſcend once more by the direct path, through the lawn, and croſs the rude wooden bridge, that is ſupported by a ſtone-buttreſs in the centre ; on paſsing over which, the view, both up and down the valley, is very elegant, crowned with hanging woods, in almoſt every direction. When acroſs the ſtream, you ſhould take the left-hand path, and follow the curve of the river, till interrupted by a brook that falls from Bwlch-Gwalter, a hill above. The path then winds up the brook, which

" Rolls in muſic down the rocky hill,"

moſt agreeably ; till arriving at a tree, thrown over for a bridge, you have a very pretty picturefque fall to the right, accompanied with graceful ſcenery of rocks, fern, long moſs, and light trees,

" Where rills amuſive ſend from rocks around,
" A ſolitary, pleaſing, murmuring ſound."

Savage's Valentine's Day.

Thence the walk aſcends a little, then grows
level

Heford 14th Oct 1786

level, and, at the firſt turning to the right, we
ſhould carefully avoid aſcending, as that is only
a branch to get a ſhorter return from the upper
walk to the houſe : continue, therefore, along
the river, as it winds through the vale, till arrived at ſome aſh trees, finely grouped, juſt
where the ſtream bends: and here, at a ſmall
gate, leave the foreſt to enter a ſtraight path,
(which ought to be covered cloſe), whence the
firſt fine view preſents itſelf up the valley ; and,
as the horizon is quite low, the Yſtwyth broad
and ſhallow, and the foreſts every way aſcending from its margin, it demands ſome attention.

The end of the ſtraight path delivers us to a
large piece of grazing-ground, of very unequal
forms ; one ſide of which hangs directly over
the river, the other climbs the hills, and melts
into the woods. Skirting this delicious meadow a little way, and contemplating the woods
which riſe directly from the oppoſite bank of
the Yſtwyth, one ſees, guſhing from them,
with a divided caſcade, the waters of the mill
brook, ſhaded with noble branches, and looſe
ſtems of wild oaks: after which the whole river
contracts almoſt ſuddenly, and retires into a
rocky channel, fringed with trees, which conduct

duct to the ftone-bridge, of one arch, mentioned in my laft walk.—Here we are led to
the right, by the path that encircles the mead,
in a gentle afcent, and foon begin to gain ex-
tenfive views in perfpective of the valley; but
near the end of the path the waving heads of
climbling forefts open grandly, giving a hint of
what one has foon to expect at a more elevated
fituation; for although the maffes fold in grace-
fully on each other, yet no part of the river is
in fight, owing to the front fcreen which firft
delivered us to this incomparable mead.

That feaft, however, is only for the prefent
delayed; for the walk now fuddenly turns up to
an artificial dam, conftructed for the purpofe of
drowning the meadows (a mode of improvement always attainable in this part of the country). This dam forms a bafon and regular cafcade, which, though little obferved here, would
in many parts of England be obferved as a confiderable curiofity; the waters coming down a
deep ravin, whofe rocks are, by the rolling torrents, wafhed fmooth and round.

Afcending this brook the path is at firft fcooped into the rocky fides of the ravin, abounding
with the moft romantic fcenery; and prefently
the

the brook or torrent is almoſt loſt, but ſoon
appears again above, alternately making little
falls at every angle.

You now paſs a mine hole ; but before leaving this, and indeed in many other places, one
ſhould look back down the rocky dingle, to
obſerve how beautifully the diſtant ſmooth hills
contraſt with its rugged bottom, and ſhrubby
ſides.

Aſcending ſtill in a tortuous path, eaten as
it were into the bank, and frequently ſuſtained
from beneath, the eye is ſoon again fixt, and
the foot arreſted, by a precipitous fall of the
whole brook about fourteen feet, pouring itſelf
ſteadily into a baſon, from between two ſmooth
rocks, with a regular loud murmur that remains
long upon the ear.

Aſcending a few paces, you come to a little
but precious caſcade, ſcattering its waters in a
triangular form, down a flat ſlaty rock, on the
oppoſite ſide of the ravin we are tracing. This
reſplendent rill might eaſily, from its ſituation
and ſcenery, be conducted into almoſt any
figure, and ſeems perfectly adapted to take the
                                                        form

form of a piſſe-vache or ſpout, as it iſſues under
a rocky head near forty feet high, and almoſt
perpendicular.

The ravin now narrows faſt, and the path
wreathes with it, when a ſmall cloſe cave is
perceived on the right; on entering which, a
roaring ſound of water aſſaults the ear, which
increaſes on advancing through the dark paſſage; when, turning ſuddenly to the left, light
breaks in, and you ſee, through a large aperture, a luminous ſheet of water, falling juſt before you, with noiſy velocity, into a deep hole
beneath. After rains this aperture cannot eaſily
be approached, as the ſpray beats in like a miſt,
and ſometimes even the torrent; but the contraſt of the gloomy paſſage you are in, with the
light of the opening, and the rapid motion of
the waters, hanging down before it like a
ſhower of iſicles, produces an effect on the
mind that is very impoſing, and reminded me
of the following lines in Chaucer's dream:

They came to the darke valey
That ſtante betwixtin rockis twey
———— werin a few wellis
Came renning fro the cliffes adowne,

That

29

That made a dedly flepinge fowne,
And renning down right by a cave
That was under a rocke ygrave
Amid the vally wonder deep.

Returning from this damp den of Tropho-
nius to the light, a frefh furprife is prepared for
us, producing a more pleafing fenfation ; for,
defcending a few loofe fteps of flate, a bridge of
two trees conducts us acrofs the torrent over a
deep channel of intire rock ; and we ·then in-
ftantly perceive the caufe of all the founds we
have heard ; for from above comes tumbling
the whole brook, precipitating itfelf from behind a fmooth rock, in the moft picturefque
form, under fome decayed oaks, white, foaming, and impetuous ; rolling at length into a
deep boiler under the bridge, and worming
its way, in irregular windings, down the
meandering vale.

No art has been ufed here, yet I queftion if
any art could improve it ; for the whole is, indeed, fit for the canvafs of the painter.

It is poffible, I believe, to return on the oppofite fide ; but, as no walk is yet marked out,
I fhould rather recommend returning acrofs the
rude bridge, to thofe whofe heads are not apt
to

to be giddy ; and, enjoying the fcene downwards, continue the walk, till arriving near a
bold piece of fmooth rock, formed like a feat,
the path takes to the left : and after continuing
round the brow of that remarkably-fmooth,
tumuloufly formed hill (of which I before took
notice, from the church of Eglwys-newydd,
and which feems to be marked out for a Druid's
temple), the aftonifhed eye is all at once
prefented with a command of the valley, that
beggars all defcription—a mighty and magnificent theatre of varied forefts, on both fides afcending majeftically from the river Yftwyth,
which rufhes through the valley in the moft
pleafingly irregular lines ; bordered here and
there with rich ftripes of pafturage ; often bend-
ing its blue courfe till loft behind the projecting
points of land covered with woods, and again
breaking out in the diftances ; the whole crowned with fmooth, verdant caps, towards whofe
fummits vegetation diminifhes occafionally
broken by gray moffy rocks that protrude from
the foil ; the whole interfperfed with rude
fhepherds' cottages, and fprinkled delicioufly
over with flocks and herds : in a word, you
fee at one view, from a proud eminence, the
whole range of this exquifite valley, extending
to Lord Lifburne's woods ; on the right, capt
by

at Hafod Cardiganshire
11 Sept 1786

6

by Grogwinian's fall; while, to the left, the bare
moſſy mountains of Sputty-Yſtwyth, terminate
the ſcene, and mingle with the vapours of the
horizon.

The impreſſion this view made upon my
mind *is indelible;* yet I ſaw it without any ad-
vantageous concomitants. What then muſt be
the effeâts of ſun-ſhine—vapours—autumnal
foliage—a fine aurora—or a clear moon light!
what, in the language of Oſſian, " When the
" blaſt has entered the womb of the mountain-
" cloud and ſcattered its curling gloom around,"
for here, on this globoſe promontory, a bard
might indeed ſit, and draw all his fine images
from nature!

Winding round the crown of this precious
knoll, ſet up as it were by art to examine the
whole ſurrounding country, you ſee in every
direâtion the abundance of the proſpeâ.

The chief entrance-road from Rhyadargwy,
Eglwys-newydd, with its ſweet poſition under
the groves, hence looks charmingly. Below
alſo, the fine ſcenery that ſurrounds the flower-
garden, with its little temple, is ſeen ſnug beneath
the

the trees, and retiring, as it were, under the wings of the wood. When fatisfied with thefe fine things, defcending gradually, and leaving the open walk again, we plunge into the foreft higher up, which had before, at our outfet, been traced below.

Here, on paffing·in, parallel to the river, with fhades above and fhades below you, and fometimes enclofed in deep foliage, the openings to the oppofite hills, richly clothed with trees, have fine effects: particularly where a little path turns down (but which you are not to follow), where the flower garden, far beneath, always pretty among fuch wild fcenery, with the promontory-like hill that peers over it, and the approach-way, that fo judicioufly fkirts it below, makes a fweet picture.

The afcent is now rather rapid. The walk foon hangs over a precipice, compelled to enter the fides of the hill, till a rude fet of ftone fteps afcends to the front of a mafs of moffy overgrown rock (that would be a good ftudy for au artift as a mere foreground) conducting us to the entrance of a cavern-way, cut through the folid mountain, which here thrufts out a promontory,

promontory, whofe fides are perpendicular, and
whofe bafe is far below ;

—— fequefter'd to the nymphs, is feen,
A moffy altar, deep embower'd in green.

Odyffey, *book* xvii. *l.* 240.

After paffing this excavated paffage, one foon
hears the found of the fall we firft met with after
croffing the river, and fees the brook gliftening
almoft under our feet ; when, turning up to
the left, along a rocky fhelf, it meets you,
fpreading into an abundance of flafhing rills,
and paffing round a little infulated fpot, fapped
by the waters, in their falling current, among
moffy ftones and tangled underwood. Here a
bridge of two flabs, rudely placed, meets the
path ; and foon after you are pleafingly furprifed
with a fine view of the manfion, dropt like a
pearl on the oppofite floping hill, in a recefs,
fo clofely furrounded by wood and rock, that
although you have been long travelling far above
it, it never meets the eye till this moment, and
now only partially ; for, continuing on a little
further from the bridge, we foon emerge from
thefe woods, on afcending a hill, and command nearly as fine a profpect up the river as
before we had downwards from *the fwelling*

C   *mount;*

mount; with the additional ornament of the houfe in the foreground: and, what is rather fingular, within ten yards of the fame fpot, turning back, there is a very original unwooded profpect of the upper fheep-hills.

A defcent, rather precipitous, now leads to the confervatory, and fruit-walls, on the oppofite fide of the river, which is paffed by a very long flying bridge. After viewing which, and the exotics, a fhort eafy afcent brings you back again to the point from which you fet out.

Dark the gigantic rocks projecting hung,
Crown'd with gray oaks, in rude diforder flung;
Thund'ring and hoarfe a fmoaking torrent fell,
Spreading a dingy wave, and foamy fwell;
Whofe rufhing ftreams in whirling eddies fweep,
Loud-founding, rapid, turbulent, and deep.

AFTER what has been already faid of the
walks about HAFOD, in which I fhall undoubt-
edly be fufpected of high-colouring, arifing
from the effects of early impreffion, it may be
imagined that the tale is told; or, at any rate,
that what follows will be but amplification: fo
far am I however from fubfcribing to fuch an
opinion, that on re-perufing my former defcrip-
tions, I find them feeble, frigid, and far infe-
rior to the fubject; and, for what is to come,
I have to regret, that not only my poor talents, but language itfelf, will fink under it; for
how are words to imprint things, when, where
nature has done much, even the art of painting,
in able hands, is feldom found adequate to the

C 2   office?

office? My plan, therefore, is, to defcribe as
faithfully as I wifh to draw; convinced that it
is better to poffefs even a middling outline of
an object that gives us pleafure, than to have a
falfe, though fine, picture; efpecially where
the beauties of landfcape are concerned, which
remain undecayed, to confront at all times the
delineation.

There is a walk from HAFOD, which, if we
knew of Milton's having ever trod, it would
enable us to account for the natural origin of
the fineft of his images *. Of that walk I
am going to attempt a defcription:

On leaving the houfe, and paffing into the
woods oppofite the plain front, by a road conducted along the fide of a hill, we foon arrive
at one of the approach-gates; where the way
goes clofe by the river Yftwyth, which is bordered on the left by very craggy, bold, and high

---

* But he, deep mufing, o'er the mountains ftray'd,
Thro' mazy thickets of the woodland fhade,
And cavern'd ways, the fhaggy coaft along,
With cliffs, and nodding forefts, overhung.

Odyffey, *b.* iv. *l.* i.

fheep-

fheep-walks ; on the right, by Mr. Johnes' elegant woods. Here a bridge* faces you, compofed of hewn native ftones, thrown over the
river in one arch, unneceffarily high, for no
flood could poffibly reach it, yet infinitely more
ornamental on that very account: it is backed
by fteep hills to the left, and, on the right,
adorned by a range of mountains, clothed up
to the very fummit with verdant forefts.

Leaving the bridge to the left,† a very little
meadow, encroaching on the woods, prefents
itfelf, overhanging the river: at the end of
which is the mouth of a deep hole, where the
eddying waters of a fmall brook feem to have
paufed, to acquire ftrength to force their exit
into the river; forming ftrange fmall bays
among the rocks that compofe its bottom, and
leaving little clods that fuftain a fingle fhrub,
or a bare ftone, whofe fides are for ever wafhed
by the rolling waters. A ruftic bridge, confift-
ing of a fingle tree, with a rail compofed of a
branch, conveys you fafe acrofs the fhaded
little torrent ; on tracing up which, among
trees, you foon arrive at a moft alluring cafcade, where the waters of this pretty brook roll
in a twifted form through a hole, high above ;

---

* Pont-rhyder-Groes.   † Here we leave the map.

over which an old ftone-arch makes the crown,
which was formerly ufed as a bridge to a mill,
but is now fo decayed as to appear like an acci-
dent of the rock : while that, through which the
water preffes, on one fide is highly ornamented
with ivy, fern, and creeper ; and, on the other,
is as richly adorned with ftraggling young
oaks, whofe long branches wave with every
wind acrofs the fall ; and, by their bright co-
lour, finely contraft the deep fhade of the hu-
mid ftone : a circularly formed boiler below receives the whole, white with foam, into its
dark bofom ; and it glides away under fmooth
flaty banks, fringed with rafpberries and fern.

A graffy fwell, intermingled with moffy
ftones, flopes conveniently before the face of
the folid cafcade, and, amidft fuch vaft furrounding forefts, makes it altogether a moft
interefting and cheerful fcene.

But all thefe pictures vanifh foon from the
memory on rejoining the river, ftruggling, and
foaming through its rocky, impenetrable bed ;
where it rufhes in under a bold, entire mountain of bare folid ftone ; whofe maffy front pro-
jects forward, fo as almoft to embrace the oppofite fteep fide of a hanging ridge of graffy
hills,

al Hafad
Cardiganshe
14 Sept 1986

hills, that prefent a narrow, irrefiftible barrier
on both fides; which confining the roaring
waters, during thaws and floods, feems to account for that formidably profound channel,
worn, by the ftream, all the way beyond it,
in forcing downwards through the deep-gullied
valley, grooving into the earth's entrails, as it
works toward the fea.

For this inbound channel is one entire, bare,
broken rock, corroded by the action of the
ftream, or ground away by the friction of its
own loofe fragments, inceffantly whirling in the
water-worn caves.

Many ancient and accidental ruins break it
finely ; as well as the wild moffy arms of
oaks, that fpring from the fiffures of the fides,
in places where no woodman has yet been dar-
ing enough to carry his axe ; convinced, that
fhould he fucceed, it would not be worth while,
at the rifque of life, to cope for the fallen timber with the fullen ftream.

Indeed the fmoothnefs of the bottom-rocks,
with their often perpendicular fides ; the cold
depth of the dark bafons beneath ; and the violence of the flood ; would render it abfolutely
dangerous

dangerous for any mortal to venture there, even
in the fummer feafon.

Thus continuing to explore the right-hand
fide of this acherontic ftream, by following the
fheep-paths through the wood, you find the
means of frequently approaching the promon-
tories of its banks, by fteep defcents, that dip
towards the margin of this terrific channel:
where, when fafely arrived, no language can
image out the fublimity of the fcenes; which,
without quite arriving at a fentiment* of averfion, produces, in the empaffioned foul, all
thofe thrilling fenfations of terror, which ever
arife from majeftical, yet gloomy exhibitions.

But, what a pleafure! after you have attained
the point of fome impending rock, covered
with long ftreaming grafs, where a little ledge
prefents itfelf, with a level footing; whence
with fecurity you can look both up and down
the caverns of this channel, to fee its flood

---

* If any one demands what I mean here, by the
fentiment of averfion, let them look down the well
at Carifbrooke Caftle, as the lighted paper defcends,
till it expires fuddenly in the cold profound.

come

come winding heavily towards you, through the gloomy, damp hollows, falling from bafon to bafon, or fpacious, or profound.

At other points we behold a rugged cave, worn, during the lapfe of ages, under the oppo-fite projecting rocks; whofe beetling brows, crowned with trees, almoft overhang and darkly fhade the deep pools whence they fprang; to the edges of which are clinched the fantaftic roots of aged oaks; from whofe fides depend flender bands of ivy, waving with every breeze, or dipping in the wells beneath; wildly fhoot-ing acrofs the whole, long, crooked branches of oaks vibrate fufpended; and, with their fcanty, but elegant leaves, chequer the fhades of the moift caves below;

" And holy horrors folemnize the fhade."
Odyffey, *b.* xvii. *l.* 245.

Judging from the vehement effects of thefe powerful waters, on the oppofite rocks, one is naturally led to fufpect that mines are worked under the bafe we ftand on: a circumftance which, united to the profpect of the treacher-ous fringe that furrounds our narrow platform, through which the eye not unfrequently pene-
trates,

trates, where all fhould feem folid, adds not a
little to the fublime and awful imaginations,
that force themfelves to our fancy, on examin-
ing the fcene around.

And when I obferved the caution with which
a dog approached thefe mouldering margins,
and liftened to the plunge of a piece of ftone
hurled into one of the pools, I felt a revulfion
that, notwithftanding the fublimity of the picture, made me fpeedily remove from the fpot.

Wandering down thefe woody dells, you at
length come to a winding path, that leads to a
ruftic bridge of three trees and a rail, projected
acrofs the dark chafm from rock to rock, where
" the river through the fhaggy hill rolls under-
" neath engulph'd;" on paffing which, a low, flat,
perpendicular rock faces you, worked by the
pick, to make a fafe landing.

Here, turning about, a thoufand romantic
objects prefent themfelves: the rural bridge—
the rocky channel it bends acrofs—the murky
fhade around—the fretful waters of the foaming
flood—the wood-crowned rocks afcending high
behind you—and the fine climbing foreft in
front, terminated above by Grogwinian's filvery
fall,

fall, fhooting through the trees, and leaping from fhade to fhade—thefe, altogether combining with the recent traces of the pictures you have juft left, fetter a penfive mind to the fpot, and force from the poet, or painter, at leaft a figh at parting.

Nor let me be faid to have overcharged the canvafs :—for " Here is the rock, and the tree,
" and the roaring ftream : here the gray ftream
" winds in the valley, and the trees fhake their
" green heads in the wind : here the aged
" oak bends over the waters, and fighs with all
" its mofs : the thiftle is there in the rock,
" and fhakes its beard to the gale : here are
" rocks broken with thunder, the ftreams of
" whofe chinks have failed."

" Hail, fifter fprings,
" Parents of filver-forded rills!
" Ever bubbling things!
" Thawing chriftal! fnowy hills!

Crafhaw, p. 1.

After afcending the hill, and paffing the
little village of Sputty Yftwyth, acrofs fome
moors, there is a walk of about three miles from
the place I have juft been defcribing, which,
though not very agreeable in itfelf, brings the
curious traveller to a rather original cafcade,
remarkable for its height, and furrounding
fcenery: the place, called Cwm-Caradoc, is
faid to have derived its name from a man who
rode into it on horfeback, and was killed, as
he well might be, by the fall.

It is produced by a brook, which, paffing
the high way, drops fuddenly, a few yards from
it, into a very deep dingle, moft beautifully ornamented

namented with trees and wild fhrubs : which
brook flows away below, under the fides of a
hill, richly embellifhed with oaks of long ftand-
ing, and fuch as are feldom found in this high
country.

At about eight miles diftance from HAFOD,
in a folitary, but picturefque valley, there is alfo,
for bold walkers, a cataract of great magnificence, and a fine painter's fall at a mill juft beyond it.

The cataract is compofed of the river
Rhyddol, falling in one vaft body into a tre-
mendous boiler, fcooped out by the force of the
waters in great floods; the whole bottom
of which is white with foam ; and which,
when the waters rife, during thaws, becomes
alarming even to the neighbours of this fpot,
who are chiefly miners and charcoal burners,
or thofe who wafh the black jack : a mineral
ufed in making brafs, and in the collection of
which many poor people are conftantly employed.

The furrounding fcenery alfo of this fpot is
very grand, being compofed of lofty mountains,
whofe fides are one continued foreft.

But

But that which renders the refidence of HAFOD the moft remarkable is, that with all its natural beauties, it is clofe in the vicinity of mountainous forefts, of a character totally different from its own; of a character, I may add, totally unlike any thing I ever before beheld, and which many people think fuperior to any place in Wales.

The region to which I allude is about thofe vallies, folding within vallies, of fides precipitous, and clothed with endlefs woods, feated at the very foot of Plinlimmon, into which the waters of the Fynach and the Rhyddol are poured, as it were, from their urns (for both are in fight at once); the former, coming down from beneath the Devil's bridge, has no equal for height and beauty that I know of; for although a ftreamlet to the famous fall of Narni, in Italy, yet it rivals it in height, and furpaffes it in elegance.

To go to it from HAFOD, you need not leave the eftate, in a part of which it lies, but, the walk is near five miles; however, you will always find refrefhment at the little public-houfe I formerly fpoke of, and which has been for that purpofe erected lately by
Mr.

Mr. Johnes, in front of the Rhyddol, and clofe to the Fynach-fall. Nor will one excurfion fuffice common obfervers; nor indeed many, to the lovers of the grand fports of nature : and, although the intended paths are not as yet fketched out, I fhall recommend to thofe who can bear the fatigue of climbing among dingles; who, in fearch of beauties, are capable of defcending from the " Hilly crofts, that brow the " bottomed glades down to the dark fequeftered " rocks below," to enter upon the Fynach-ftream, about four miles from HAFOD, and fkirt it, as well as they can, down to the Devil's Bridge. To do this, I will fairly confefs, that (in the prefent ftate of things) they muft creep often through thickets " dank or dry;" fome-timetimes encounter, " the undergrowth of " fhrubs and tangling bufhes;" " tempt the " fteep glade," treacherous with flaty ruins; pafs over " rocks with frowning brows; be " loft in leafy labyrinths, and thickeft fhelter " of black fhades embowered;" but then in reward for all this, I can fairly promife them, (for I experienced thofe pleafures fully), they fhall as often find themfelves in

   " Umbrageous grots and caves of cool recefs,
" over which the ivy creeps;" behold " the
              " murmuring

" murmuring water falls down the flope dell
difperfed," or " in a glaffy pool unite their
ftreams ;" fee " crifped brooks, with mazy
" error under pendant fhade, offering their
" glaffy, cool, tranflucent waves ; midft grots
" and caverns, fhagged with horrid fhade ;" and
as a fpecimen of thefe fcenes, I would have fub-
joined two out of twenty fpots, in a fpace lefs
than a mile, on this romantic ftream ; comput-
ing from the flate quarry, and water-mill under
Mr. Hughes's farm, to the Devil's bridge ; beneath the dreadful double-arch of which the
future walks are intended to be conducted, fo
as to bring the fpectator fuddenly, as by enchantment, into the front of that incredibly
ftupendous chafm of intervolving vallies, clothed to their mifty top with wood of—" Thickeft
" covert, interwoven fhade, a verdant wall ;"
beneath, the receptacle of many waters, the
principal of which is the Rhydol, ftrongly
marked by the foaming cataract, and the broad
boiler that receives it ; but too diftant below
for its roaring tide to be audible by day.

As to the Fynach, its fall is fo nearly perpendicular beneath the Devil's Bridge, and it
has fo far to travel down to what is called the
Devil's Hole ; that, to view it in all its detail,

it

it is neceffary to crofs the bridge, and go round
to the point of a mountain; whence, as from a
ftage, the whole lies delightfully expanded.

After paffing deep below the bridge, as
" through a narrow firth, with noifes loud and
" ruinous," into a confined chafm; the fleet
waters pour headlong and impetuous; and,
leaping from rock to rock, with fury, *literally*
" lafh the mountain's fides:" fometimes almoft
imbowered among deep groves, and flafhing at
laft into a fan-like form, they fall rattling
among the loofe ftones of the Devil's Hole;
where, to all appearance, it fhoots into a gulph
beneath, and filently fteals away: for fo much
is carried off in fpray, during the inceffant re-
percuffions it experiences, in this long tortuous
fhoot, that, in all probability, not above half
the water arrives at the bottom of its profound
and fullen grave.

Thus I have brought the reader to the end of
my detail, and to a point where I may well
be difpenfed with; for it is not only beyond my abilities to enter into a full relation of
the fcenes about this place, but quite unnecef-
fary, for all are now before him, expanded under the admiring and aftonifhed eye—and never

D   eye,

eye, I will venture to affirm, beheld thefe fcenes without aftonifhment : I fhall therefore only fay, at parting, from the divine poet I have fo often quoted—that thefe hills like

———————————————— Paradife,
Now nearer crowns with her enclofures green,
As with a rural mound, the champion head,
Of a fteep wildernefs ; whofe hairy fides,
With thicket overgrown, grotefque and wild,
Accefs denied; and overhead upgrew
Infuperable height of loftieft fhade ;
A fylvan fcene ; and, as the ranks afcend
Shade above fhade, a woody theatre.
——————————— Thus lovely feemed
That landfcape, and of pure, now purer air,
Meets the approach, and to the heart infpires
Vernal delight and joy, able to drive
All fadnefs but defpair.

MILTON, b. ix.

F I N I S.

at Hafod Cardigan Shire
11 Sep.r 1786 –

ERRATA.

The Reference to the Note in Page 5, ſhould be at *knowing how to chuſe*, in Page 6, line 3.

Page 7, line 15, for *fuzzy* read *furzy*.

Page 9, in the note, for a comfortable *in*, read *inn*.

Page 16, line 2, for *the* pretty caſcade, read *a* pretty caſcade.

Page 21, line 7, read admit *of* a path.

Speedily will be published, in One Volume, Quarto,

THOUGHTS on OUTLINE, SCULPTURE, and the SYSTEM that guided the ancient Artists in compofing their Figures and Groupes.

Accompanied with free Remarks on the Practice of the Moderns, and liberal Hints cordially intended for their Advantage.

To which is added, *Twenty-five* CLASSICAL DE-SIGNS, compofed on the Principles recommended by the Author, G. CUMBERLAND.

Alfo, Author of ANECDOTES of JULIO BONASONI; The POEM of LEWINA the MAID of SNOWDON, and BRITISH LANDSCAPES.